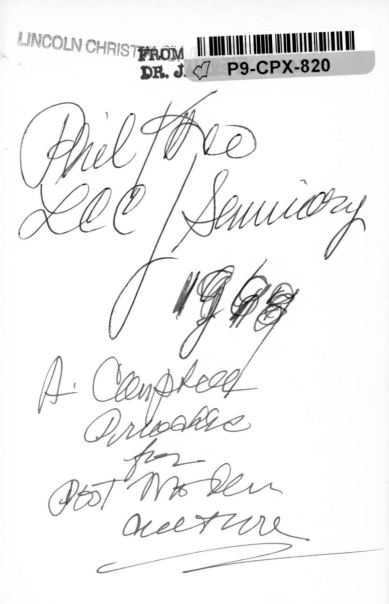

ALEXANDER CAMPBELL
AS A PREACHER

Alexander Campbell as a Preacher

By

ARCHIBALD McLEAN

Author of

"Where the Book Speaks"

BAKER BOOK HOUSE

Grand Rapids 6, Michigan

1955

Library of Congress Catalog Card Number: 55-9472

A reprint of the edition
printed in 1908 by
Fleming H. Revell Co.

ALEXANDER CAMPBELL
AS A PREACHER

Alexander Campbell as a Preacher

A LEXANDER CAMPBELL was a many-sided man. He was an author and editor. Sixty volumes have his name on their title pages. He founded a college and was its president for a quarter of a century. He taught regularly all those years. He was a defender of the faith as he held it. He had oral discussions lasting for days with John Baptist Purcell, a Roman Catholic bishop; with Robert Owen, of Lanark, the Secularist; and with several other of the strong men of their time. He had written discussions with sceptics, Jews, Unitarians, Universalists, Baptists and Pedo-baptists. These discussions covered nearly all questions relating to Christian doctrine and to church polity. Mr. Campbell was a man of affairs. He married and raised a family. He was the father of fourteen children. He managed a large business and made money. He served the state that adopted him. He was a member of the constitutional convention of Virginia. He sat in council with ex-President Madison, with Chief Justice Marshall, with Randolph of Roanoke, and with many other of the illustrious men of the old commonwealth. Mr. Campbell was a conversationalist worthy to rank with Luther and Johnson and Macaulay and Coleridge. He preached in most of the states of the Union, in Canada, and in Great Britain and Ireland. It is as a preacher that he is considered in this study.

Mr. Campbell was ordained January 1, 1812. It is safe to say that he was one of the best known and most effective preachers of his own or of any time. While he lived in Bethany, where his business was conducted and where the college he founded was located, he travelled much and preached everywhere. The announcement that he was to preach seldom failed to call together a throng too great for any building. When the weather permitted, he spoke in the open air to the thousands that assembled from near and from far. Much of his preaching was done on what was then the frontier. The Western country was sparsely settled. Religious privileges were not as abundant as they are now. The people were hungry for the bread of life. No man even in a metropolitan pulpit spoke to more intelligent or responsive audiences. Like most of the preachers in the wilderness, Mr. Campbell was an extemporaneous speaker. The pioneers liked men, as one of them said, " who could shoot without a rest." While making the most conscientious preparation for the pulpit, he wrote but little. Writing sermons was exceedingly irksome and distasteful to him. At that time newspapers were not as numerous and as enterprising as now; reporters were not as ubiquitous nor as accomplished. Because of these facts, few of Mr. Campbell's sermons have been published. Only two or three have **Few Sermons Preserved** been preserved; and these are not verbatim reports. While he was in his prime it does not appear that it ever occurred to him or to his friends that those sermons upon which he bestowed so much thought, and into which he put so much of his life, and which he preached with so much power, should be taken down and printed for the information and edification of those who might wish to know more of his message and style and to think his thoughts over after him. It is nothing less than a calamity that those sermons which produced such profound and far-reaching results should have perished forever when their author died.

Mr. Campbell's sermons cannot be placed in evidence. The most that can be done is to gather up some of the recorded testimony of those who heard him. Fortunately, these are a great host. Some of the witnesses, whose words shall be cited, were eminent in their day and will be famous for all time. Some were his students in the college; they heard him often. There are no better judges of true preaching than a body of bright young men gathered from all parts of the world. When we are told of impressions that lasted for half a century and longer, we may be sure that the sermons were of exceptional excellence.

Jeremiah Sullivan Black heard Mr. Campbell at different times through a series of years. Mr. Black was for a time Chief Justice of Pennsylvania. Later he was the Attorney-General of the United States. He was one of the foremost lawyers and advocates of the nation. He heard Mr. Campbell first in his youth. Happening to be in Wellsburg when Mr. Campbell was to preach, he went to hear him. He took his stand upon the steps of the court-house. At the close of the sermon he found himself inside the railing and within a few feet of the speaker. He had been drawn insensibly and unknown to himself. He told Mr. Campbell how much he had been impressed with what he had heard. Not long after, Mr. Black made a journey from Somerset, Pa., to what is now Bethany, W. Va., to hear more and to make a confession of his faith in the Christ and to be baptized. Many years later, Judge Black said: " As a great preacher, he will be remembered with unqualified admiration by all who had the good fortune to hear him in

Impressions on His Hearers

the prime of his life. The interest which he excited in a large congregation can hardly be explained. The first sentence of his discourse ' drew audience still as death,' and every word was heard with rapt attention to the close. It did not appear to be eloquence; it was not the enticing words of man's wisdom; the arts of the orator seemed to be inconsistent with the simplicity of his character. It was logic, explanation and argument so clear that everybody followed without an effort, and all felt that it was raising them to the level of a superior mind. Persuasion sat upon his lips. Prejudice melted away under the easy flow of his elocution. The clinching fact was always in its proper place, and the fine poetic illustration was ever at hand to shed its light over the theme. But all this does not account for the impressiveness of his speeches, and no analysis of them can give any idea of their power."

Ex-President Madison testified to the same effect. He said: " It was my pleasure to hear him very often as a preacher of the Gospel, and I regard him as the ablest and most original expounder of the Scriptures I have ever heard."

Robert Graham, some time president of Kentucky University, and himself a most effective speaker, spoke thus of Mr. Campbell: " I can hardly express my admiration of him in every walk and employment of life. In the social circle he was by far the finest talker I ever heard; in the lecture-room, the most instructive; and in the pulpit I am sure he had few equals, and no superior, according to my standard. He charmed all alike, the old and the young, the educated and the uneducated. Indeed, no one could listen to him and not confess him to be one of the greatest men of his age. He had a style of his own, and always elicited the admiration of his hearers. He drew and held his audience till they seemed oblivious to the passage of time. I have heard him speak for over two hours at a time, and yet no one became weary." President Graham was educated at his feet. He heard " the old man eloquent" as a pupil, and later when his own judgment was more mature, and this is his testimony :

> " Time but the impression deeper made,
> As streams their channels deeper wear."

James S. Lamar, of Georgia, a prolific author and a gifted speaker, gives his estimate of Mr. Campbell as follows : " People would come from far and from near to hear him, some of them making a day's journey. Others would follow him from place to place, so as to hear him from day to day. The difficulty generally was to procure a house that could accommodate the crowds that flocked to hear him. The people admired him, loved him, hung enchained upon his lips, quoted him, trusted him, and spread his name and fame wide and far. But he was *sui generis.* He did not belong to that class that is commonly meant when we speak of popular preachers. He did not preach like them. He filled and moved in a sphere of his own. He seemed to have, and deeply to feel that he had, a special mission, an appointment from his Lord to do a peculiar and world-wide work. I believe that the divine Spirit so rested upon his soul that he lived and thought and preached under the sacred and solemn pressure of this conviction. If, therefore, he was popular, it was not because of the orator's art; not because he amused and pleased the fancy, or touched and stirred the shallow emotions, but because all that was holiest in men's hearts and aspirations, and most clear and unclouded in their intellects, recognized the grandeur and divinity of the objects which he set before them; and they loved to move with his lofty spirit in the region where Christ was truly recognized as Lord indeed, and honored and trusted to His very last word and ordinance as the true Messiah, the Son of the living God." This is the testimony of a man of taste and discrimination, of a man who heard Beecher and Spurgeon and the other popular preachers of their time. Mr. Lamar speaks of Mr. Campbell as a great man—God-appointed and God-inspired. He represents him as " a figure statuesque, colossal, mighty ; a grand and masterful man ; worthy of his sacred mission, worthy of the great brotherhood whom he led into the light and liberty of the Gospel, and worthy of the large place which he will one day be given in the history of the Church."

Dr. Heman Humphrey, then president of Amherst College, heard Mr. Campbell twice. In his account of what he saw and heard, he said : " In listening to him you feel that you are in the presence of a great man. He speaks like a master of assemblies, one who has entire confidence in the mastery of his subject and his powers, and who expects to carry conviction to the minds of his hearers without any of the adventitious aids on which ordinary men find it necessary to rely. There were many fine and truly eloquent passages in the two discourses I heard, but they seemed to cost him no effort, and to betray no consciousness that they were fine." Referring to the second sermon, Dr. Humphrey said : " He dwelt chiefly on the two clauses of the text, ' Justified in the spirit, received up into glory,' and I can not in justice refrain from acknowledging that I never remember to have listened to or to have read a more thrilling outburst of sacred eloquence than when he came to the scene of the coronation of Christ, and quoted the sublime passage from the twenty-fourth Psalm, beginning, ' Lift up your heads, O ye gates, and be ye lifted up, ye everlasting doors, that the King of glory may come in,' when he represented all the angels, principalities and powers of heaven as coming together to assist, as it were, in placing the crown upon the Redeemer's head."

Theodore S. Bell, then a young man and afterwards a distinguished physician in Louisville, heard Mr. Campbell preach a sermon based on the first chapter of the Epistle to the Hebrews. In that sermon the speaker dwelt on the divine glory of the Son of God, a theme upon which he was always surpassingly eloquent. Dr. Bell said: " I never had heard anything that approached the power of that discourse, nor have I ever heard it equalled since. Under the training of my mother, one of the most thorough scholars in the Bible that I ever knew, and of Dr. Fishback, although I then made no pretensions to Christianity, I was almost as familiar with the Bible as with the alphabet. But that speech on Hebrews lifted me into a world of thought of which I had previously known nothing. It has been forty-five years since I heard that pulpit discourse, but it is as vivid in my memory, I think, as it was when I first heard it." Wherever he spoke, he impressed people in the same way. One Baptist preacher said what many others felt : " I once thought I could preach, but since I have heard this man I do not seem, in my own estimation, to be larger than my little finger."

Mr. Campbell's style was his own. He did not aim to copy any of the famous orators of ancient or modern times. One of the strong pioneer preachers of Kentucky told him that he was surprised to find in him an entire want of gesture and mannerism; that he talked as men commonly talk. Mr. Campbell told him that he had studied the arts of elocution, but had conscientiously refrained from making any use of them. " The apostles were sent out as witnesses to a certain great fact. Suppose that one of them should, in making his statement before the people, have plied his arms in gesticulation, stamped his foot in vehemence, and declared his testimony in the ears of the people in a loud, stentorian voice? But how weightily fell the words of those first preachers, when, with composure of manner, natural emphasis, and solemn deliberation, they spoke forth the words of truth and soberness." President Humphrey noted that there was nothing vociferous or impassioned in his manner. He said: " I think he is the most perfectly self-possessed, the most perfectly at ease in the pulpit, of any preacher I ever listened to, except, perhaps, the celebrated Dr. John Mason, of New York. No gentleman could be more free and unembarrassed in his own parlor."

Isaac Errett, the founder and for many years the distinguished editor of the *Christian Stand-*

ard, spoke thus of Mr. Campbell: " We have known him, in his prime, stand for two hours, leaning on a cane, and talk in true conversational style, with scarce a gesture in the entire discourse. But to a fine personal appearance and dignity of manner, he added a clearness of statement, a force of reasoning, a purity and sometimes a pomp of diction, a wealth of learning, a splendor of imagination, and an earnestness often rising into impassioned utterance, which clothed his pulpit efforts with a high degree of oratorical excellence."

Isaac Errett's Estimate

There is a tradition in Bethany to the effect that, when the students went out to preach, they carried canes and leaned on them while speaking. In his later years Mr. Campbell wore a long patriarchal beard. The students encouraged their beards to grow long.

It was said of Mr. Campbell by a competent critic that his style was transparently clear—his argument perfectly understood and appreciated by all—and yet his language was largely Johnsonian. " The Latin and Greek derivatives were so familiar to him and so wrought into the very fibre of his thought and mind, that, coming from him, they seemed not strange and foreign, but near and homelike. His hearers might not always have been able to define all the words he used, but they saw and felt what was wrapt up in them.

Style and Language

Thus it was that learned and unlearned listened with rapture to his preaching, notwithstanding he was at no pains to accommodate his language to lower grades of intelligence. Not only did they hear with delight, but his thought was deeply imbedded in their minds, to be retained and treasured there, to be solemnly reconsidered and pondered, changing in many cases the very currents of life, and leading to a blessed and glorious destiny."

It was said of Chalmers that his delivery was the first and second and third excellence of his oratory. " On great occasions he was absolutely terrible. His heavy frame was convulsed; his face flushed and grew Pythic; the veins of his forehead and neck stood out like cordage; his voice creaked or reached to a shriek; foam flew from his mouth in flakes; he hung over his audience, menacing them with his fist, or he stood erect, maniacal and stamping." The effect was tremendous. Whitefield's preaching was as when the strong wind passed by and rent the mountains. Hume acknowledged that his eloquence surpassed everything he had ever seen or heard in any other preacher. He said that it was worth walking twenty miles to hear him. His elocution was perfect. " His face was a language, his intonations music, and his action passion." Garrick said Whitefield could make men weep or tremble by his varied utterances of the word "Mesopotamia." Whitefield had absolute control of the passions of immense audiences. "When he was in the pulpit every eye was fixed upon his expressive countenance; every ear was charmed with his melodious voice; all sorts of persons were captivated with the propriety and beauty of his address." Franklin was so delighted with him that he said he would rather hear him tell what was false than to hear any one else tell what was true. Of Robert Hall it is stated that when he spoke, "breathless silence prevailed." As he grew more animated, five or six auditors would rise and lean forward over the front of the pews; a new sentiment or expression would cause others to rise, till long before the close it often happened that a considerable number were standing. The concluding appeals of his sermon on "Dead in Trespasses and Sins" were remarkably sublime and awful. Dr. Ryland hastened part way up the pulpit stairs, and while tears trickled down his venerable face, exclaimed with a vehemence which astonished both the preacher and the people, "Let all men who are alive in Jerusalem pray for the dead that they may live!" Duff left the pulpit as if he had been dragged through the Atlantic. His tall, ungainly form swayed to and fro, and his long right arm waved violently, and the left one hugged his coat against his breast, his voice raised to the tone of a Whitefield, and his face kindled like one under inspiration. He went home drenched with perspiration and wrung his clothes. Of John Knox it is affirmed that he seemed as if he would "ding the pulpit into blads and fly out o't." There was nothing in the least dramatic in Mr. Campbell's manner. He rarely made a gesture of any sort. There was no attitudinizing; no nervous flourishings; no pointing upward to the stars; no stretching forth of outspread arms as if to embrace mountains. He was seldom tender or pathetic. His style reminded some of the apostle as he reasoned with the people from the Scriptures, opening and alleging that the Jesus whom he preached was the Christ. It reminded others of the Master as He sat on the mountain or in the boat, and spoke as man never spake to those who sat around Him on the mountain or on the shore. When Mr. Campbell spoke, there was no gesticulation and no sign of perspiration and no beating of the pulpit. He did not alarm any by the way he pronounced certain words. His reliance for effects was upon the inherent power of the truth he was illustrating and enforcing, and upon the Spirit of God.

It was said by Henry Ward Beecher that no one can describe to you the lightning flash of an excited eye, the thunder of a mighty voice, the manifold evidences of the surging feelings that roll out from an orator and submerge the hearers, as the waves roll in from the deep and cover the beach. Something of that kind was seen in Patrick Henry. It is recorded that, attracted by

Beecher's Description of an Orator

some gesture, struck by some majestic attitude, fascinated by the spell of his eye, the charm of his emphasis and the varied and commanding expression of his countenance, juries lost sight of the law and the facts and their duty, and the judges bathed in tears perverted equity, and the people carried the orator in triumph on their shoulders. Mr. Campbell never sought to carry the minds of his auditors by stratagem or by assault. Nothing would have been gained by such a victory as Patrick Henry won over judge and jury. Mr. Campbell sought to inform and to persuade.

Marvellous effects were produced by the preaching of Edwards and Wesley and Whitefield and Erskine and Christmas Evans and others, both

Effects of Preaching

in Great Britain and in America. The effect of one of Jonathan Edwards' sermons was as if some supernatural apparition had frightened the people beyond control. They were convulsed in tears of agony and distress. Amid their tears and outcries the preacher paused, bidding them to be quiet that he might be heard. The reading of the text in another case caused the auditors to feel that they were slipping into the pit, and they seized the pews and pillars to save themselves. By all accounts, Edwards had some awful and electrical power. Speaking of the effects of the revival which grew out of his own ministry, he said that " nature often sank under the weight of divine discoveries, and the strength of the body was taken away." The person was deprived of all ability to walk or speak. Sometimes the hands were clenched and the flesh cold, but the senses remained. Animal nature was often in a great emotion and agitation, and the soul so overcome with admiration, with a sort of omnipotent joy, as to cause the person, unavoidably, to leap with all his might with joy and mighty exultation. Under the preaching of Wesley, some sank down, and there remained no strength in them: others exceedingly trembled and quaked. Some were torn with a sort of convulsive motion in every part of their bodies, and that so violently that often four or five persons could not hold them. Hearers dropped on every side as if thunderstruck. Wesley speaks of one woman who was held in bed by two or three persons. " It was a terrible sight. Anguish, horror, and despair, above all description, appeared in her pale face. The thousand distortions of her whole body showed how the dogs of hell were gnawing at her heart." " Another tore up the ground with her hands, filling them with dust, and with the hard trodden grass, on which I saw her lie with her hands clenched as one dead." Another roared and

Physical Manifestations in Early Revivals

screamed as in a more dreadful agony. Some
continued lying on the ground for two or three
hours, as if actually dead. Whitefield tells that
on one occasion the whole church was drowned
in tears ; they wept and cried aloud as a mother
weeps for her first-born. Another time the vast
congregation was drenched in tears. When he
preached to the colliers the tears made white
gutters down their black cheeks. Copious weeping followed his ministry. Thus it is said that the
people were so greatly afflicted that the room
was filled with cries ; and when they were dis-
missed they went home crying aloud through
the streets to all parts of the town. Again he
says, that shrieking, crying, weeping and wailing
were to be heard on every corner ; men's hearts
failing them for fear, and many falling into the
arms of their friends. Many were carried away
when he spoke, as wounded soldiers are carried
away from the field of battle. " The Word was
sharper than a two-edged sword ; and their bitter
yellings and groans put me in mind of the wail-
ings of the damned in hell."

In the great revival in Kentucky and Tennessee
early in the last century, people fell like a log on
the floor or on the earth or in the mud, and appeared as dead. They lay helpless and apparently
lifeless for hours. In many instances the head
would be jerked backward and forward, and from
side to side, and so quickly that the features

could not be distinguished. In this operation the head touched the ground behind and before. Saints and sinners were thus affected. Men cursed the jerks while they were thrown to the ground with violence. Some danced till nature was exhausted, and they fell prostrate to the floor. In addition to the jerks, there was the barking exercise, and the laughing exercise, and the singing exercise, and the running exercise and the falling exercise. It is stated that persons on the way to the meeting would bark like spaniels, and sometimes during the services they would start up suddenly with a fit of barking, rush out, roam around, and in a short time would come barking back. The preaching of Christmas Evans in Wales was characterized by the jumping exercise. To be sure, these were not the sole nor the main results of the preaching of these famous men. Souls were born into the kingdom of God, and saints were instructed and built up on their most holy faith.

When Mr. Campbell preached, these bodily agitations were conspicuously absent. There were no swoonings or trances or roarings, no running against a wall, no beating themselves against the ground or tearing it up with their hands, no screamings or ravings or other evidence of mental derangement. The effect was perhaps as great, but it was different. He talked

Absence of Bodily Agitations When Campbell Preached

to the assembled thousands as an advocate talks
before the Supreme Court of the United States.
There were no convulsions or contortions. But
many of those that heard gave themselves then
and there to the Lord. Others resolved to mend
their ways and their doings. Others, still, went
home to search the Scriptures to see whether the
things they heard were true. The results of Mr.
Campbell's preaching might be recorded in the
language of the New Testament. "Many of
those that heard, believed, and were baptized."
Judge Riddle, speaking of his preaching and the
effect of it, said there was no appeal to passion,
no effort at pathos, no figures of rhetoric; but
a warm, kindling, heated, glowing, manly argument, silencing the will, captivating the judgment, and satisfying the reason.

Robert Richardson, the biographer of Mr.
Campbell, describing his power over audiences,
says: "Nothing, indeed, was more striking than
his singular ability to interest his
hearers in the subject upon which he
treated. With this his own mind was
occupied, and, being free from all thoughts of
self, there was in his addresses an entire absence
of egotism, and nothing in his delivery to divert
the attention from the theme on which he dis-
coursed. For the first few moments, indeed, the
hearer might contemplate his commanding form,
his perfect self-possession and quiet dignity of

Ability to
Interest

manner, or admire the clear and silvery tones of his voice, but these tones soon filled the mind with other thoughts. New revelations of truth, themes the most familiar invested with a strange importance, as unexpected yet obvious relations were developed in a few simple sentences; unthought-of combinations; unforeseen conclusions; a range of vision that seemed to embrace the universe and to glance at pleasure at all its varied departments—were as by some magic power presented to the hearer, and so as to wholly engross his perceptions and his understanding. While that voice was heard, nothing could dissolve the charm. Minutes became seconds, and hours were converted into minutes, so that the auditor became unconscious of the lapse of time, and his attention during the longest discourse was never weary. Without any gestures, either emphatic or descriptive, the speaker stood in the most natural and easy attitude, resting upon his innate powers of intellect and his complete mastery of the subject, impressing all with the sense of a superior presence and a mighty mind. His enunciation was distinct, his diction chaste and simple, his sentences clear and forcible. The intonations of

Voice and Emphasis his clear and ringing voice were admirably adapted to the sentiment, while by his strong and bold emphasis upon important words he imparted to what he said a peculiar force and authority. . . . His power was thus derived, not from graceful action, gesture, nor from flowery language, nor elaborate or glowing description, nor merely from logical argumentation, but from his singular faculty of stating and connecting facts—of producing more novel and striking combinations of related truths, and of evolving the grand fundamental principles of things. Seizing upon these by an intuitive faculty of sagacity, he obtained at once the complete mastery of the subject, which he was enabled to disengage with the greatest ease from all its complications, as the experienced woodman, skillfully placing his wedge in the heart of the timber, rives it through all its knots and windings, or as some Napoleon directs at various distant points large and isolated bodies of troops, whose destination cannot be determined by ordinary minds until the unexpected concentration of the whole upon a given point reveals the comprehensive genius of the warrior."

While Mr. Campbell's style was conversational for the most part, there were times when he spoke with the utmost fervor. Thus one of his pupils says that sometimes he was like a living fire or a sweeping tornado, forcing you to forget all idea of logical connection, and impressing upon you only the idea of power. At such times he

At Times Fervor and Power

spoke with a rapidity and fervor of utterance
which literally defied phonography, and so enchained the mind and heart as to paralyze the
hand that would otherwise have reported his
every sentence. He convinced his auditors;
he did more than that—he stirred them. On
one occasion it is said, when he was addressing
one of the most intelligent audiences that ever
assembled in Kentucky, quite a number of highly
gifted and educated men rose unconsciously to
their feet and leaned forward towards the speaker,
as if fearing to lose a single word that fell from
his lips; and what made the case more remarkable was that many of them were public advocates of the views he was assailing, as being, in
his judgment, contrary to the Word of God;
yet such were the force, clearness and eloquence
that he brought to his task, that even those who
differed from him could not but pay this high
tribute to his admirable powers of close thought,
and of lofty and brilliant expression. W. K.
Pendleton, his successor as president of the college, said: " His ideas flowed on a perpetual
stream—majestic for its stately volume, and
grand for the width and sweeping magnificence
of its current. With a voice that thrilled with
the magnetism of great thoughts, and a person
imposing and majestic as his mind was vigorous
and commanding, no one could hear and see him,
and fail to discover that he was in the presence

of one on whom nature had set the seal of transcendent greatness." While enriching his discourses from his vast stores of knowledge, and presenting them with great power, the impression of immense *reserve* of force was always left upon the hearers.

To some, Mr. Campbell did not appear to be a great pulpit orator. Whether he was or was not depends upon the meaning we give to oratory and eloquence. Longinus said that A Great Pul- an orator must have a vehement pas-pit Orator sion, a certain madness, a divine phrensy, breathing into his thoughts, and inspiring his speech. Aristotle gave it as his opinion that eloquence or oratory is the power of speaking on any subject that which is most persuasive. Whitefield had the "vehement passion." His sermons are commonplace. Apart from him they have little merit and little power. Those sermons that now seem so tame were, when delivered by him, like a volcanic eruption—like torrents of red-hot lava, that carried everything before them. When Chalmers rose to preach, the entire assembly set themselves for the treat that was coming. They were all eager and intent. Every breath was held, every cough suppressed, every fidgety movement settled. When the sermon closed and the great preacher said, " Let us pray," there was a hurried rush for the aisles and the doors. Those that came not to worship God, but to enjoy the fascination of human eloquence, did not care to remain for the benediction. When he was the lion of Glasgow, Chalmers felt that he made a mistake in going to that city, for he could hear of no good that was being done by him. He was as one that had a lovely voice and could play well on an instrument; the people heard his words, but they did .not do them. The church that was so mightily stirred by the preaching of Edwards drove him out into the wilderness to preach and teach the Indians. Mr. Campbell attracted great audiences. He held them firmly in his grasp. He sent them away deeply impressed. This shows that oratory is no one stereotyped thing. If it be true, as Aristotle held, that persuasive speech is oratory, then Mr. Campbell was one of the greatest pulpit orators that ever lived. It was noted in his time that he spoke largely to men, to lawyers, physicians, teachers and editors.

At home Mr. Campbell spoke from an hour to an hour and a half. Abroad and on special occasions he spoke twice as long. He often spoke two or three times a day. The length of his sermons was in harmony with the customs of the time, and barely met the expectations and wishes of the people. They were hungry and wanted a full meal. His biographer states that minutes became seconds and hours became minutes. The people were so entranced that they were unaware of the lapse of time.   A noted Baptist minister said to a friend, at the close of one of Mr. Campbell's sermons, that it was a little hard to ride thirty miles to hear a man preach thirty minutes.   His friend said: "It has been longer than that; look at your watch."   On looking, he found that it had been two hours and a half.   He said: "Two hours of my time are gone and I know not how, though wide-awake all the time."   That was no uncommon experience.   The people were so engrossed with the great theme under consideration that they forgot all else.   His sermons were so clear in statement, cogent in argument, rich in diction, and forcible in illustration, as to hold his auditors in rapt attention to the end.

Mr. Campbell's style of sermonizing was as peculiar as his delivery.   He did not believe much in what is known as textual preaching.

Textual Preaching

He said that half a century ago the greatest divine was the man that could bring the most doctrine and pronounce the most sermons from a clause of a verse.   He told of a Scottish divine who preached a sermon to a company of beer drinkers from the word "Malt."   The plan of the sermon was: First, explain the different figures of speech in the text; secondly, exhibit the fourfold effects of malt in this life; thirdly, declare its fourfold effects in the life to come; fourthly, deduce a few practical

instructions and exhortations for the benefit of
the hearers. In discussing the first head there
were four topics suggested by the four letters—
M, A, L, T. Thus *M* suggested *metaphorical;*
A, allegorical; L, literal, and *T, theological.*
Under the second head there were four particu-
lars setting forth the effects of malt in this life,
and all suggested by the text, as follows: *M,*
murder; *A,* adultery; *L,* lasciviousness; and *T,*
treason. Under the third head showing the effects in the life to come were these, and all suggested by the same letters; *M,* misery; *A,* anguish; *L,* lamentation; and *T,* trouble. The
fourth head yielded four exhortations and all
based on the same text; *M,* my dear hearers; *A,*
all of you; *L,* look diligently; *T,* to yourselves,
to the text, and above all to abstain from the use
of M-a-l-t liquors.

Another preached a sermon from the word
" But." Naaman was a mighty man of valor,
" but he was a leper." He spoke of the excep-
tions in human life. It was a trial sermon and
very ingenious and eloquent. After it was over
the officers of the church said to him, " Brother,
you are a very interesting preacher, *but* you are
not the man we are seeking." Another spoke
from the text, " And." " Philip *and* Bartholo-
mew." Yet another spoke from the exclama-
tion, " Oh ! " and said a number of pretty things
about it. One spoke from the mutilated text,

" There appeared a great wonder in heaven, a
woman." Mr. Campbell could make nothing of
such fantastic texts. He spoke on the great
themes that run like rivers through all Scripture.
His aim was to set forth what the Word of God
taught, and not to prove that it is true, or that
some notions held were true because they are
supported by texts of Holy Writ. With him
the Scriptures were authoritative and final.
His purpose in all his preaching was to make
known the mind of the Spirit. Our minister
went to hear him to discover whether he was
a Calvinist or Arminian. After hearing him,
he was asked if he found where
Back to Christ Mr. Campbell stood. He said, " No,
I know nothing about him ; but, be he
devil, or be he saint, he has thrown more light on
that Epistle and the whole Scriptures than I have
heard in all the sermons I ever listened to before."
He went back of Calvin and Arminius and
Athanasius to the apostles and their Lord. He
was a profound and life-long student of the Scriptures. His familiarity with the language of the
Bible enabled him to employ its glorious expres-
sions and beautiful similes with great effect. " It
was from it, indeed, that his discourses derived
their convincing truths, their inspiration and their
grandeur. Bible themes, Bible thoughts, Bible
terms, Bible facts, were his materials, and these
he wrought up with consummate skill into intel-

lectual and spiritual palaces of glorious beauty, in which every auditor desired to prolong his stay. For the embellishment of these he employed Scripture metaphors much more frequently than comparisons, but it was upon analogies that he seemed chiefly to rely for illustrations as well as for argument. These, constituting his chief imagery, were usually grand, far-reaching and wide-spreading. Scriptural facts, precepts and promises seemed to be connected with them as naturally as flowers and fruits with the trees of the orchard. Uniting with their means the present with the past, one dispensation or institution of religion with another, and earth with heaven, he enlarged every one's conceptions of the plans of the infinite Creator in the remedial system, and through his varied and striking associations of thought produced the most profound and indelible impressions."

Mr. Campbell had a message for his generation. He was engaged in a movement that had for its object the union of the people of God upon the basis of the Holy Scriptures, to the end that the world may be evangelized. He called no man master. He honored the long line of saints and confessors and reformers. He learned what he could from each of them. But he did not make himself a follower of any or call himself by the name of any. No one of these had been crucified for

A Message for His Generation

him, and he had not been baptized into the name of any one of them. He went back to Christ and to His inspired apostles, and set aside all human creeds and confessions and dogmas that claimed to be authoritative. His voice called the people back to Christ and to the teaching of the Scriptures as the all-sufficient and alone-sufficient rule of faith and practice. He felt that as long as Christians continued to rally around human standards there would be division and confusion and every evil work. He saw in Christ, and in Christ alone, the one true rallying-point for all believers. In his preaching he sought to exalt Christ: this was his sole and supreme aim. He held Him up as the only Saviour and rightful Lord of all men, and urged them to pay the most punctilious regard to all His precepts and ordinances. Among his favorite themes

Favorite Topics were these: The coronation of Christ; the mystery of godliness; the glory and dignity of the Christ; the riches of the saints. On no other subject was he so eloquent and grand and enrapturing as on the glories, the majesty and superhuman dignity of Christ Jesus. The last sermon he ever preached was on the glory of the Redeemer and the completeness of His salvation. Christ was the core of all his preaching—His character, His offices, His perfection, His supremacy. The Messiah was his perpetual and his highest delight. To him Christ was all and

in all.   No other preacher ever held more firmly
to the essential deity of our Lord.   No one ever
sought more consistently and continuously to set
Him forth as the only hope of men and nations.
To his thought Christ was the key of all human
history.   In his conversation this was the master
topic.   No matter where he began, he soon found
himself talking about Christ and His salvation.
As all roads led to Rome, so all subjects were
connected in his thought with Christ.   His conversation was relieved with bursts of eloquence
which even his finest flights in the pulpit never
surpassed.   On his death-bed he asked of the
friends that gathered about him :   " What think
ye of Christ? of His divine nature ? of His glorious
mission ? of His kingly office, the sovereign Ruler
of the heavens and the earth, the Fountain of
universal being ? "   Shortly before his spirit left
the scene of his toils and triumphs, some one re-
marked that the sun was rising.   He answered :
" But to you that believe on His name, the Son
of Righteousness shall arise with healing on His
wings."   He felt what Tennyson expressed :

> " Our little systems have their day,
>   They have their day and cease to be ;
>   They are but broken lights of Thee,
>   And Thou, O Lord, art more than they."

In his youth he preached a sermon in which
he contrasted the Gospel with the law of Moses.

His text was: " What the law could not do in
that it was weak through the flesh,
Sermon on
the Law   God, sending His own Son in the
likeness of sinful flesh and as an offer-
ing for sin, condemned sin in the flesh." The
sermon was preached in the open air, to an immense concourse of people. Mr. Campbell stood
upon a rock while he spoke. His plan was as
follows: 1. Ascertain what ideas we are to
attach to the law in this and similar portions of
the sacred Scriptures. 2. Point out those things
which the law could not accomplish. 3. Show
the reason why the law could not accomplish
these objects. 4. Illustrate how God has reme-
died these relative defects of the law. 5. Deduce such conclusions from these premises as
must obviously and necessarily present themselves to an unbiased mind. He undertook to
show that Christ is superior to Moses, and the
Gospel to the law. He combated the idea, then
so common, that in every conversion there must
first of all be a work of the law. The sinner
must hear the thunders of Sinai before he was in
a condition to hear the pardoning voice of the
Son of God. Mr. Campbell held that Mosaism
was provisional and local. It was for one people
and for one age. It had no glory because of the
more excellent glory of the Christian system.
He never denied or doubted the value or the
permanency of the ethical element in Mosaism.

That element was taken up and incorporated in the Christian system. But, as a system, Mosaism waxed old and long since passed away. The shadow gave place to the substance, the type to the antitype. Mr. Campbell was careful to distinguish the different dispensations. He spoke of the patriarchal as starlight; of the Jewish dispensation as moonlight; of the mission of John the Baptist as twilight; of the Christian dispensation, beginning with the reign of Christ and the descent of the Holy Spirit, as the sunlight of the world. The patriarchs had the bud; the Jews had the blossom; we have the mature fruit of divine grace. This sermon was thoroughly evangelical. But because of it, Mr. Campbell was tried for heresy. Some narrow men sought to drive him out of their communion.

Tried for Heresy In the trial he proved too much for his opponents. They continued to persecute him for years. Thirty years after this sermon was delivered it was published. Mr. Campbell said that so great had been the change of public sentiment in that time, that no association would take exception to its doctrine. No man could be further from being an antinomian.

Isaac Errett summarized Mr. Campbell's teaching as follows: " Christ, the only Master; involving a rejection of all human names and leaderships in religion. The Bible, the only authoritative Book; necessitating a denial of the authority of all human creeds. The Church of Christ, as founded by Him, and built by the apostles for a habitation of God through the Spirit, the only institution for spiritual ends; logically leading to the repudiation of all sect religions as unscriptural and dishonoring to the Head of the Church. Faith in Jesus, as the Christ, the Son of God, and repentance towards God, the only prerequisites to baptism and consequent church-membership; thus dismissing all doctrinal speculation and all theological dogmata, whether true or false, as unworthy to be urged as tests of fitness for membership in the Church of Christ. Obedience to the divine commandments, and not correctness of opinion, the test of Christian standing. The Gospel the essential channel of spiritual influence in conversion; thus ignoring all reliance on abstract and immediate influence of the Holy Spirit, and calling the attention of the inquirers away from dreams, visions and impressions, which are so liable to deceive, to the living and powerful truths of the Gospel, which are reliable, immutable and eternal. The truth of the Gospel, to enlighten; the love of God in the Gospel, to persuade; the ordinances of the Gospel, as tests of submission to the divine will; the promises of the Gospel, as the evidences of pardon and acceptance; and the Holy Spirit, in

Teaching Summarized

and through all these, accomplishing His work of enlightening, convincing of sin, guiding the penitent soul to pardon, and bearing witness to the obedient believer of His adoption into the family of God." Mr. Campbell's theology was preëminently Biblical and Christological and Christocentric.

Phillips Brooks defined preaching as truth through personality. Emerson has the same thought. He maintained that there is no eloquence without a man behind it. Mr.

A Great and Good Man Campbell's preaching would never have had the influence it had unless he had been a great and good man. Moses E. Lard, one of his scholars and himself one of the most effective preachers in America, said that nature had been lavish to Mr. Campbell. " Physically, not one man in a thousand was so well endowed. Nature was in a fertile mood when she molded his large and sinewy body. Material was abundant and bestowed with no grudging hand. There was not a pound of flesh too much, nor a pound too little. As to resources of the mind, no word but opulent will describe him. Here he was preëminently great, in the true sense of the word. His head was faultless, the finest I ever saw." Mr. Lard placed him among the very first of the very greatest of the sons of men. Mr. Campbell's father was a profound classical scholar and a born teacher. He took as much pains with his son as James Mill did with his son, John Stuart Mill. Mr. Campbell took a course in Glasgow University. He developed and disciplined his mind by diligent study. For many years he spent sixteen hours a day in his library. In this case, reading made a full man. In his discussion on infidelity his opponent came to the end of his resources long before the time came for closing. Mr. Campbell went on and spoke for twelve hours on the Christian religion. This is one of the most remarkable addresses ever delivered.

Education and Study

Perhaps no man ever knew Mr. Campbell that denied his greatness. It was said of Burke that no one could stand with him under a bridge in a shower without discovering that he was no ordinary man. As Mr. Campbell walked the streets of London, a man who did not know him said : "There goes a man with enough brains to govern Europe." In his presence other men were silent, and left him to do all the talking. They instinctively paid homage to the power of his intellect. College men are quick to see and recognize a great man. They spoke of his majestic and commanding presence. After fifty years they still feel concerning him as they did while under the spell of his genius.

No one ever called his character in question. His critics assailed his views; no man ever had enemies more in number or more venomous. He was accused of all kinds of heresies.

Character He was charged with holding views that were mutually exclusive. His reputation was without spot. His bitterest enemies failed to find a flaw in his character for truth, integrity and goodness. His life was above suspicion and above reproach in that fierce light that beats upon a leader of men and blackens every blot. No father could wish for an only son a career more splendid or more stainless. To those that knew him well he was most cheerful, gentle, genial, just and devout; and as dearly loved for his goodness as he was venerated for his greatness. Mr. Campbell lived in constant and conscious fellowship with God and

Religious Life with Jesus Christ. Like Enoch and Noah, he walked with God. He was filled with the Spirit. He prayed with his family and with his domestics. He was never too busy or too weary for family worship. This was a cardinal feature of his household economy. He had little confidence in a piety that was not nourished and instructed by the daily study of the word of God and a perpetual habit of prayer. Thus sustained by divine assistance, he labored for fifty-four years with an energy and a fidelity never surpassed.

This study may fitly conclude with the testimonies of four men of renown. Judge Black said of him: " The life of a Christian man worthy of his vocation is a battle at best. He of whom I speak contended valiantly for the faith once delivered to the saints, not only against natural allies of Satan, but against errors which appeared to be consecrated by the approbation of good men; creeds imbedded in prejudice; falsehood guarded by interest which the slightest disturbance infuriated. It was a war against principalities and powers and spiritual wickedness in high places. The little band of disciples that gathered around him at first, and the world in derision called by his name, were as literally the 'sect' everywhere spoken against as their predecessors in primitive times. To effect a great reformation under such circumstances; to convince large numbers against their will; to organize the believers into a compact and powerful body; to conquer the respect of the world—these are proofs of intellectuality and moral force with which only a few of the children of men have been gifted. To these qualities were added an unfailing courage, a fortitude that nothing could shake, a chivalrous sense of justice to his opponents and affection for his friends, second only to his love for the cause to which he devoted his life. What higher claims can any man set up to the character of a hero?"

George D. Prentice, the brilliant editor of the

Louisville *Journal,* after hearing Mr. Campbell, wrote in his paper as follows: "Alexander Campbell is unquestionably one of the most extraordinary men of our time. Putting wholly out of view his tenets, with which of course we have nothing to do, he claims, by virtue of his intrinsic qualities, as manifested in his achievements, a place among the foremost spirits of our age. His energy, self-reliance and self-fidelity, if we may use the expression, are of the stamp that belongs only to the world's first leaders in thought and action. His personal excellence is certainly without a stain or shadow. His intellect, it is scarcely too much to say, is among the clearest, richest, profoundest ever vouchsafed to man. Indeed, it seems to us that in the faculty of abstract thinking—in, so to say, the sphere of pure thought—he has few, if any, living rivals. Every cultured person of the slightest metaphysical turn who has heard Alexander Campbell in the pulpit or in the social circle, must have been especially impressed by the wonderful facility with which his faculties move in the highest planes of thought. Ultimate facts stand forth as boldly in his consciousness as sensations do in that of most other men. He grasps and handles the highest, subtlest, most comprehensive principles as if they were the liveliest impressions of the senses. No poet's soul is more crowded with imagery than his is with the ripest forms of thought. **Surely** the life of a man thus excellent and gifted, is a part of the common treasure of society. In his essential character he belongs to no sect or party, but to the world."

Bishop Hurst says that few men have impressed themselves more profoundly on the religious life of their age than Alexander Campbell. "His personality was of the most vigorous type, and for over a generation his name was a tower of strength over the whole United States. He was a man of purest character and the highest consecration. He leavened the whole country with his views. Few men have exerted a wider influence."

Referring to Mr. Campbell, General Robert E. Lee quoted the words of Dr. Symonds spoken about Milton: "He was a man in whom were illustriously combined all the qualities that could adorn or elevate the nature to which he belonged; knowledge the most various and extended, virtue that never loitered in her career nor deviated from her course. A man who, if he had been delegated as a representative of his species to one of the many superior worlds, would have suggested a grand idea of the human race." The New York *Independent* has said that there is not a religious body in Christendom that, whether it will confess it or not, has not been profoundly affected by his life and work. His influence and fame since his death have increased rather than diminished. It is believed by many that they will continue to increase till that for which he contended so long and so earnestly and so ably will be realized, and there will be one flock as there is one Shepherd. Coming generations will rank him among the greatest of the many God-given men that have blessed our earth.